T0197736

Lord Bid Me Come Unto You

Shaaron Wheeler

AuthorHouse™
1663 Liberty Drive
Bloomington, IN 47403
www.authorhouse.com
Phone: 1-800-839-8640

© 2011 Shaaron Wheeler. All Rights Reserved.

No part of this book may be reproduced, stored in a retrieval system,
or transmitted by any means without the written permission of the author.

First published by AuthorHouse 09/22/2011

ISBN: 978-1-4670-4192-8 (sc)

Printed in the United States of America

Any people depicted in stock imagery provided by Thinkstock are models,
and such images are being used for illustrative purposes only.
Certain stock imagery © Thinkstock.

This book is printed on acid-free paper.

Because of the dynamic nature of the Internet, any web addresses or links contained in this book may have changed
since publication and may no longer be valid. The views expressed in this work are solely those of the author and do not
necessarily reflect the views of the publisher, and the publisher hereby disclaims any responsibility for them.

authorHOUSE®

Dedication

This book is dedicated to those men and women of God that poured encouraging words and prayers endlessly into my life. Too many to name you know whom you are! I am forever grateful and thankful and I love you all!

I wish to thank one of my spiritual sons Robert Burns

"Shawn" who jumped in to help design my cover!

"The Lord gave the word and great was the company of those that published it" Psalm *68:11(KJV).*

FOREWORD

Philippians 4:8

New International Version (NIV)

8 Finally, brothers and sisters, whatever is true, whatever is noble, whatever is right, whatever is pure, whatever is lovely, whatever is admirable— if anything is excellent or praiseworthy—think about such things.

I thank the Almighty God for the life of my wonderful sister in Christ Mother Shaaron for allowing the Holy Spirit to lead her in putting this book together. At such a critical time when the body of Christ even the strong are falling Shaaron is staying strong for God.

I thank God for this book that has come to reveal the things of God "Lord Bid Me Come Unto You".

It is a book you need to read to strengthen your faith.

God Bless Love Your sister

TABLE OF CONTENTS

The message of the morning glory shower . . . .

As I bathed getting ready for work and began to thank God for my upcoming marriage, a glimpse of one of my married friends crossed my mind. She didn't seem so happy. The Lord said to me, "I have given you the keys to tell the older women who are married and the embers have seemingly gone out of their marriage how to rekindle the flame. I am here to ignite the fire, start, poke the embers and to restore the flames", sayeth God. These words are not my own trust me, I was not thinking about anyone else while bathing, but that is just how good of God we serve is. He not only thinks about the Esther's of the world, those women who are in preparation for their upcoming mates, their kings, but God also thinks about the married woman, the Hannah's that cried out before the Lord, so I believe these words from God are for them!

God said, "why would I leave you out?" You have entered into the covenant place beyond the veil that I want to take my new daughters of Zion. Your strength and perseverance seeking me has not dwindled away. You must recapture what it took to get to me and pursue, overtake and recover all. The same is with your marriage. The things you did to catch My eye, the things you did to make Me take notice of you, the things you did to make Me bid you to come unto Me.

Your steadfastness and delight in preparing yourself for Me . . . . what happened to that?"

So many of you, my daughters who have come beyond the veil before, now sit gloomily before Me not at all concerned about how you look. I still want to know that you desire Me. I still want to know that I am first in your life. I still want to know that the fire you once had for Me is still burning, still roaring like a forest fire consuming everything in its way as you come unto Me. Because you were heavy laden and I told you I would give you rest (Matthew 11:28 KJV)

Now my daughters come to the "king" that I have sent to you the same way. (meaning the man God placed in your life). He had bid you come unto his rest years ago. What have you done to keep him calling unto you? The deep calleth unto the deep.

(Luke 4:11NIV) the Lord tells Peter, the expert fisherman, "launch out into the deep")

Have you launched out to set sail to come unto him again? I prepared a place for you a haven for your love. Have you just taken it for granted? Oh yes, I will forever be there because I am GOD, but my man servant, the "king" whom I have prepared for you is only human. Now my daughter, I will take you once again behind the veil and show you how to restore, fan the flame and rekindle the fire!" sayeth God.

NO.1 BE CONFIDENT

Know that without a shadow of a doubt, it was I who called you and my word says a voice of a stranger they shall not follow"

(John 10: 5, 27KJV) Remember, he only has eyes for you, but the enemy is busy trying to get into the holies of holies where you are to destroy and because satan can not, he will try and cause confusion in the outer court (1 Corinthians 14:33 KJV)

NO.2 TIMING

Set a specific time to come unto ME. Time is of the essence. I am a God of infinity as with my son. You should know his hours of operation. I God operate all the time, but a human can only call you when they are thinking about you so you must put yourself on the "king's" mind. Smile more at him, and less conversation about whatever. Let him fantasize about what is keeping her so happy. He will believe it is him. Hum around the house singing praises.

NO.3 POSITION

Make sure that the coast is clear. Sometimes, we have to affect our atmosphere. My word says, "that the woman with an issue of blood would not be denied." She said, "if I may but touch His clothes, I shall be whole (Mark 5:28KJV) She became radical in getting what she knew she needed. Once in His presence, she confessed her desire and it was well received. You see, when you pursue with faith and tenacity believing that you will succeed without a shadow of a doubt then it shall come to pass. You will be accepted for your truth and Jesus said to the woman who touched him, "daughter thy faith has made thee whole, go in peace and be whole of thy plague".

(Mark 5:33KJV) Your husband may not say that in so many words, but he will hold you closer realizing that a strong effort was made to try to reach him. Women of God it is a spiritual thing!

NO.4 OUTWARD APPEARANCE

Dress the part! Esther was pampered for one year. (Esther 2:12KJV). You have had several years to be with the King. DO not lose our glow. Go back for reinforcements. Go back to the barracks and restock your weaponry. Use whatever you have. A good soldier always retreats to regain strength and supplies and then goes back out again.

HAIR

Style your hair in a way that would be suitable for your face and body and then also attractive to him. A man likes it when his woman gets compliments from other people men and woman alike. God is proud when we get praise for how we look and act more like what He created! He Has jewels in heaven, sparkle, class and ingenuity. (Revelation 12: 8-21KJV) For some of you, how many years of having children, overeating, neglect have taken over the temple of God. (1 Corinthians 3:16, 17KJV). The Holy Spirit is just that a spirit, He will dwell. Now some men look on the outside, some have not yet learned to see as God sees.

BODY

Address the body issue. Go all out on being healthy. The battle can be won a lot quicker if you were in shape. Your armor must be flawless. Start with washing your navel. I did not know why the Lord said that, but then he said, "it is connected to your life line. When you were born, the navel was the pathway for all the food and the waste to pass thru" (umbilical cord). For such a small place, God is emphasizing that no area should be left untouched. Bathe yourself in oils and sweet swelling things. Try different ones and see which ones can be attracting to his nostrils. He may comment and say, "honey what is that I smell"?

Remember that your king, like God is attracting many because of the anointing, but only the assigned, YOU, can get in. Only you, the bided one can come in. Only the legalized one YOU, can come in Counterfeits are not allowed! Your body is the temple of God and the Holy Spirit dwells within you, let God arise in you and your enemies be scattered, (Psalm 68:1KJV) Make sure your breathe is minty fresh. Remember if you have not come "behind the veil" in a while, the road may be longer, but through your desire, prayer and laying out before the chamber, you will be hear, noticed, beckoned and received for your efforts.

Now that you are behind the veil, go to work. Make sure that the kings feet are washed while yet praying silently "the steps of a righteous man are ordered by the Lord: no one place will he go and be comfortable unless in the chamber of the holies of holies with me his handmaiden, his helpmeet. Your husband, the king will think that you are honoring him; which you are, but you are using God given wisdom in the supernatural to bring forth favor from the king! Hallelujah! Esther faster and prayed and when she appeared, she was bid to come. Know that without a shadow of a doubt, God is still behind the scenes working to make your marriage fire alive, but God can only use what is given and allowed for him to use. Open your heart and hear what the spirit of the Lord is saying to your church (Revelations 2:7KJV). In this time of attack on marriages, we women of God must join forces together and share the wealth of the word of God and the wisdom of the word to bring about change, Godly structure and rejuvenation into our marriages. So through our maturing in the word, we can keep what the Lord has given to us and be joyful about it. It is a must that we fulfill the assignment God has given unto us. (Joshua 24:15KJV) We must go in with the mentality that for God I live and for God I die. Will you lay down your life for a brother as Christ did? Can you stop looking at yourself and make your husband your assignment and achieve victory where God will get the glory. Will you take off the mask of false happiness and let the tears flow and wail before God (Jeremiah 9:17NIV.) Some of you have because my heart has been pricked in the spirit and I feel the pulling of your cry in my soul, my habitation. I promise in the next few words to give you all that you have been trying to pull out of me in the spirit, by the leading of the Holy Ghost. It is my desire that not only my upcoming marriage succeed as God has ordained and purposed, but that we as a united front of daughters of Zion will accomplish the task that God has assigned to us. We will survival and we will obtain victory through Jesus Christ. The word of God says, "we overcame by the word of our testimony and the blood of the Lamb". I love you my sisters!

Chapter 2

True Worship . . . .

Now I will address, as God allows, my single sisters, handmaidens of which I am one. Our first love MUST be Jesus Christ!

Through worship know that our Father is reaching out to us just as much as we are reaching out to Him. When you get the revelation of being in His hand waiting to be escorted as his bride, his daughter, his lover, then you know that you have gone past the holies of holies. He is not sitting at the table in the holies of holies; He has not sent angels to guide you in. He has reached out His own hand from His chamber of glory to pull you in. Tell the Lord, "there is no other love like this love, of you Father, reaching out to me". There is a level you must be on to get God to respond like He does, reaching for you! This must be a personal encounter only if you have intimacy with Him. You must tell Him, "no other man, woman or child, nothing means more to me than you Father". Everything I've asked in the past doesn't mean anything now. It's just you I want; no material thing can take your place. I know now of your love for me, your undying unconditional love for me. When I smell you, your presence causes me to want to flee to be with you, my lover. On the job at my desk, needing to go to a quiet place to give you the love you are requiring through my praise. When I feel your touch on my shoulder, I know it is you my King, wooing me to come to you. And then when I am still and close my eyes, I see the sky and out of it comes a brilliance of reddish yellow orangeish light, sort of like an early sunset and puffy clouds all around and a hand, God's hands protrude out of the clouds ready to pick me up to come to make love with me. There is nothing like it. All women and men need their lover. The comfort of Him, then all is well, all is okay. Even when nothing is wrong, He'll come for you because he misses your face, your touch, your soft words, your smile. He misses your voice saying, Yes my Lord; I do love you with all of my heart, mind, body and soul. There is nothing I wouldn't do for you. You are the butterflies in my stomach. You are my everything and I need you, I do need you". God loves to hear us tell Him, "don't ever leave me my love". It is at this time, like me, you can say, "I am finally experiencing the love of my lover who has always been there. He is the one for me! He is the one for me! He is truly the one for me! He is the man of my dreams! He is my knight in shining armor and His name is Jesus and I love Him unconditionally"!

Chapter 3

How To Get To That Level . . . .

Everyone should have an altar set up in their home. Even if you don't have an extra room for a "prayer room". As a suggestion to get started, you can set aside an area in your bedroom exclusively for the Lord to come and "visit" with you. I live in an apartment right now and in my bedroom on one side of my bed is a small end table, a bible, a pad and pen. I've also included pictures of loved ones there to pray over along with other important things I have taken before the Lord. I have a comforter on the floor along with a pillow and my favorite stuffed animal. This place should only be for your meetings with the Lord. Of course, you can pray anywhere and everywhere in your home, but it is very important to God to have a special place set aside totally and exclusively for Him! My altar is symbolic of the "holies of holies" place within the temple. Each of you may have your own ideas, but hear what the spirit of the Lord is saying to you regarding your personal altar area and do just that.

What moves you moves God. He created you in His own image. If it is music, get a song of worship that feeds your spirit that says the things to God you want to say. Learn those words, learn the names of God, call them out and let Him know that you know Him and that you want a deeper relationship.

Tell God, "Lord I want to come where you are", "bid me to come where you are". You can't do this once a week, this must be done repetitiously throughout the weeks. (Ephesians 5:20KJV) You must get into the habit of knowing the "call" for you to come. Focus on scriptures that come to life in your situation. When I was going thru my healing process or seeking God to heal me from cancer, I sought out all scriptures talking about healing. I posted them on the mirrors and doors leading to various rooms. I kept the "healing" word ever before me. You might be saying, "those scriptures have nothing to do with love. They do! Jesus Christ was "wounded for our transgressions, bruised for our iniquities and the chastisement of our peace was upon Him, and by His stripes we are healed". (Isaiah 53:5KJV)

Jesus laid down His live so we could have a chance at eternal life. If that is not love, then I don't know what is! "Love covers a multitude of sins (1Pet4:8KJV) Once you are persistent in coming to the sacred place set up for you and God to meet at our home, He will come and meet you there, same time, same place. You may cry uncontrollably or just plain pass out and be taken in the "spirit realm" on a "travel" with the Lord. He may take you into the "holies of holies" and show you off to the inhabitants there. God is actually validating His love for you when He comes and visits. It is something that can't really be explained. I can only give you what happened to me before God came and took me in His arms . . . . I was engaged in a conversation and praying with someone on the phone who was in another city. Near the end of the conversation, he said, "sister, I must go now, I have company". Even though we were having a wonderful discussion about the Lord and His word, when he realized God was coming and he felt the presence of Jehovah Shammah (God is There) saw His glory, I nor the Godly conversation didn't matter anymore. All he wanted was to be with His love. When he released me from the line, I heard God tell me to lie down as well. When I did, I distinctly heard angel's voices singing. I leaned out of the left side of my bed and looked into my son's room across the hall, but adjacent to mine and his CD player was off. The sounds of singing I heard was from heaven. I lay on my back on my bed and just drifted off thanking and praising God on my breath. I knew through our prayers, praise and worship, the Lord was pleased and chose to visit Raphael and myself in His own special way. The Lord can woo you to Him while in the midst of a prayer with your prayer partner. I believe that everything having to do with getting closer to God and Him revealing Himself has everything to do with the time and season that He chooses to visit with you. Even if you don't have any of these types of experiences, God is a God who is unique and will design a special time just for you. He may choose any way He likes to come to you. Just be glad that the Lord would even consider you worthy enough to visit. Just know that the visitation that I experienced will never be forgotten as so will yours. It is forever etched in my soul and my heart that God loved me so much to consume me with His love and allow me to live and testify about it. To God be the Glory!

I have tried under the unction of the Holy Spirit to share with married and single women my experiences with our Father and also to give practical suggestions on how to reach "a degree beyond" and enter into His glory. The word of God says that He is no respecter of persons (Acts 10:34KJV) so it is up to you to pursue Him with all tenacity as you want your destiny and purpose to be fulfilled! Seek after His glory! With much agape love may God continue to fulfill His desires thru You!

Printed in the United States
By Bookmasters